Run Walk Enjoy

A Guide To Exercising Properly

© 2018

Herstellung und Verlag:

BoD – Books on Demand, Norderstedt.

ISBN: 9783748156055

Table of Contents

The Reasons Why I Wrote This Booklet

By now, virtually everyone knows the famous Czech long-distance runner Emil Zatopek, who coined the phrase "Birds fly, fish swim, men run". Equally well-known are the stunningly positive effects of a sportive lifestyle on the mental and physical health of human beings. As I see it, there is no need discussing this all over again. The reason why I have written this book and why I recommend reading it is another one: the average human being of today is one who spends most of their lifetime sitting – in the car, at the office, in front of the television screen. It can be claimed that many people have become estranged from physical work and exercise. Most so-called diseases of civilization can be attributed to a lack of exercise, a lack of movement. This fact, too, is no longer disputed so that it is not necessary to further promote this topic.

However, what is still commonly unknown is that a lot of people who have come to the conclusion that they must change their lifestyles tend to make mistakes during the transition period. Quite often they want to achieve too much in too short a time, which leads to all kinds of injuries. This, in turn, leads to frustration and not infrequently to giving up the newly set goals.

With this book I aim to help avoiding mistakes in the conversion to a sportive and healthy lifestyle.

Unfortunately, I had no such advice at hand when I became a runner myself. I had to learn by trial and error and only God knows how many times I did the wrong thing and ended up sidelined by injury. Dear reader, I am positive that you can learn a lot from my mistakes and from my advice so that you will manage the transition to a runner, jogger or walker free of pain.

I will describe in narrative form what I did right and what I did wrong. I want to motivate you to carry on and harvest all the fantastic and enriching experiences of becoming a runner/walker. This is certainly also of interest for those who want to take part in running or walking competitions.

Moreover, I will provide advice and tips for a targeted performance training because, in my experience, competition - to put it graphically - is the salt in the soup of training.

If you insert a competitive run/walk every now and then, you will most certainly derive pleasure and motivation from it. Competitions, races are concrete, palpable, experiential targets and thus a great help to stick to the new lifestyle.

In a competition you do not only get to know your own body better but you will also meet other runners, sportsmen and -women, there will be an exchange of ideas, experiences and stories, which sometimes results in a life-long friendship.

What enables me to help you to successfully switch to a healthy, active lifestyle, is my personal background of a runner - I have been running and walking for more than 40 years now - and my pedagogical background as a teacher, college principal and running club manager. I myself started running systematically when I was 29 years old - too late to become a world-class runner, but that was not what I was reaching for anyway.

I have won numerous regional championships in long-distance running, from the 5 K to the marathon. The 5K I ran in 15 minutes and a few seconds, the half marathon in 1:09 hrs and the full marathon in 2:26 hrs.

In order to provide others with helpful advice and tips, it is not necessary to have been a world class runner or rather sportsman yourself. Many of the best coaches in basketball, soccer and other sports were only mediocre considering their athletic performance.

Undoubtedly, there is a difference between being a peak performer in a certain field and the ability to teach others to become top providers.

Now that I have become a veteran runner, the proportion of walking outweighs that of running in my personal training. The borderlines between walking, powerwalking, 'wogging', jogging and running are somehow fluent and, in my booklet, I tend to use the concepts of running and walking synonymously. I often use them both, divided by a slash to show how close they are to each other.

Turning Point – How I Became A Runner

Over and over again it happens that one comes to a crossroads in life.

> *Two roads diverged in a yellow wood,*
>
> *And sorry I could not travel both*
>
> *...*
>
> *Two roads diverged in a wood, and I—*
>
> *I took the one less traveled by,*
>
> *And that has made all the difference.*

The first two and the last three verse lines of Robert Frost's famous poem *The Road not Taken* epitomize such a situation.

I personally experienced such a crucial moment when I was 29 years old. That was back in 1980, the year of the Moscow Olympic Games. At that time, I was in Southern Germany and not far from the town where I lived, the German championships in the marathon took place. Waldkraiburg was the name of the small town that staged the event. As I had nothing better to do, I went to watch the race. It was a relatively warm Sunday in April and the temperatures made it really tough for the runners. I vividly remember the runners crossing the finish line. I would not say it was exactly a pretty sight. Emaciated, with distorted faces, some of them hardly able to maintain a proper running form, they reached the channel to the finish line. But, hardly had they crossed this finish line, when the expressions on their faces changed drastically. An aura of contentment and happiness radiated from them and the strains of running 26.2 miles in really warm weather conditions vanished.

These happy faces made me take up running again and a first positive side effect was that I almost immediately stopped smoking because running and smoking are absolutely incompatible.

A second effect that pleased me enormously was that a few weeks after I had started running systematically, I fit the old pants again.

Maybe it was a mere coincidence that I defeated a fellow club runner in a cross-country running event at Waldkraiburg about a year later. I had never been able to beat him before, always finished way behind him. But from that day on it was he who finished after me, I never lost a race against him anymore. To defeat him I had to get over an inner pain threshold, which I had failed to accomplish before. But once you have succeeded in controlling this burning, drilling muscle pain, things look much better and soon you will be prepared to go through this chore again.

One more thing: a year later I ran my first marathon in 2:32 hrs.

The author completely exhausted (but extremely happy) after his victory over a fellow club runner he had never defeated before ...

> ...
>
> *I took the one less traveled by,*
>
> *And that has made all the difference.*

I can only fully underline what Robert Frost has written. Taking the turn to an active lifestyle may be the less traveled path, because it may seem the less convenient one, but it is actually worth taking it.

The First Step Is Always The Hardest

Admittedly, it is really difficult to start running or any other sports activity if you are not accustomed to covering distances on foot from early childhood on. Astonishingly enough, in our age even children tend to suffer from a lack of exercise because they do not have to walk any more. Parents or buses take them to school, where they spend most of the day sitting, hopefully paying attention to teachers and when they are back home, they often will have to do homework.

This is what modern children's everyday life looks like. Sitting and listening to someone makes you tired and consequently, you spend your free time in front of the computer or mobile phone screen playing games that are supposed to blow away tiredness.

Me, too, I often did not feel like doing a workout after a long and tiresome work day. What helped me to surpass my lower instincts, my inner laziness, were mainly three things:

a) I felt guilty when I failed to work out, when I missed a training session.

b) Joining a neighborhood running club brought a breakthrough for me. Running and walking together with like-minded people was like a drug for me. Exercising in a group made everything seem easy and it was the motivational factor I needed most.

c) Every now and then we took part in a race so that we had a fixed goal in our minds, which kept us going even if the going got tough.

From the day I had become a member of a running club I never had motivational problems again. On the contrary, I was over-eager, too keen on exercising so that I demanded too much from my body and soon had to deal with injuries and pains.

I suppose that quite a few fitness and exercise addicts striving for the modern 'model body' have made similar experiences. Bullet points: six-pack, thigh gap, sexy buttocks and so on.

On the one hand, the motivation to achieve the ideal of a slim, muscular body is a good thing, no doubt about that, because it helps to overcome the aforementioned downsides of a modern lifestyle but, on the other hand, the danger that motivation turns into addiction must not be underestimated.

The modern ideal of the slim, well-defined body is a superb motivator because in the mirror and on the scales, success can be seen and measured and that endorses and strengthens motivation additionally so that there is the danger of eating disorders or over-training, which both lead to undesired results, e. g. injuries or metabolic disorders.

Therefore, it still applies what already the Ancient Greeks knew:

The right measure is the goal.

In my booklet I will help you find out what the right measure, the right amount of exercise is.

The Initial Woes and Injuries

From the lack of motivation to hyper-motivation - this is how the path of many beginners may be described. If you have managed to run, work out regularly, you will realize very quickly what tremendously positive effects exercising has on your body and mind.

The feeling of relief, for instance, has mainly physio-logical causes: together with the sweat you work up you get rid of many toxic substances. This unburdens your kidneys and other internal organs and you lose weight, you are relieved in the literal sense of the word. When you work out, all organs of the body get better supplied with blood, i.e. they are also better supplied with oxygen, which leads to an improved general condition. The prerequisite is that you do not run too fast, but at the pace of a slow jogging. A rule of thumb regarding the right pace is the so-called speech-test tempo, which means that you must be able to talk while jogging or walking without getting into oxygen deficiency.

With a lot of beginners, who I coached in various running meets, I have seen that the initial euphoria may lead to the strong wish that they want to experience the good feeling which originates from the running body and mind as often and as intensively as possible. Thus, many runners increase the frequency, the range and the intensity of their workouts too fast and, often in all three areas at once. This inevitably leads to physical reactions because the body needs time to adapt to new challenges. The mind is willing during this initial euphoria, however, the "flesh", the body, needs periods of recovery, which are often denied to it.

I also made these rookie mistakes, but, unluckily, I did not have a coach or trainer, only my teammates who made the same mistakes, partly out of ignorance, partly out of false ambition.

What we had at our disposal as sources of information and what we read eagerly were the books of the former long-distance guru, Dr. Ernst van Aaken[1], whose core messages are still fully valid today.

_____

[1] http://dr-van-aaken.com/index.htm

Currently, there seems to be a new trend, the so-called slow jogging propagated by a certain Prof. Hiroaki Tanaki[2]. "Slow Jogging" does not mean anything else but "slow endurance running", which takes us back to the above-mentioned Dr. Ernst van Aaken who claimed that (slow) jogging is kind of a panacea for man. He taught that already in the early 1950's but met strong opposition from within the mainstream of medical men in those days who claimed that anybody who is injured or ill only needs rest, nothing but rest. Dr. van Aaken was the first to get a patient with a known history of heart attacks to run a complete marathon.

No wonder that his findings and methods of treatment were not welcomed by his fellow physicians and the pharmaceutical industry since telling someone to turn to an active lifestyle in order to stay healthy is not as profitable as treating patients by means of operations and prescribing drugs.

Back to the typical mistakes beginners are inclined to make: I was able to treat my first injury successfully

---

[2] https://slowjogging.wordpress.com/about-us/

myself. After a long run with a new pair of shoes, the tendon under the longitudinal arch of my right foot hurt like hell. I treated the painful area with a simple rolling pin I used for gentle massaging. It hurt a lot at the beginning, but I realized that the pain decreased bit by bit and after two weeks I was rid of the injury. Nowadays, fascia rolls are sold at a high price for treating injuries like the one described above and for massaging your muscles, tendons and ligaments, but you can get the same results employing the common rolling pin that can be found in every kitchen.

Running in pain is certainly not a safe business. My experience is that if the pain disappears during exercise, you are already on the way to healing. If the pain becomes stronger, then stop immediately, I repeat, stop immediately, otherwise you can seriously harm yourself and aggravate your physical condition.

The same is relevant if you have any respiratory problems. Sometimes the body just wants to tell you that it needs a break. Listen to your body and rest. Scientists have found out that it is primarily during the periods of rest in which the body prepares itself for the next level of performance. This process is called supercompensation[3].

Another typical injury commonly experienced by runners is Achilles tendonitis. In case of a real inflammation, i. e. if the tendon is swollen and reddish, only professional treatment and a certain period of abstinence from exercising can help. If the tendon is just irritated, you can also try to treat yourself by massaging the tendon with ice cubes and by gently stretching the tendon.

When I started running in the early 1980s, going to the doctor's was extremely unpleasant for many runners, because Dr. van Aaken's findings had not yet become common knowledge, on the contrary, his view of the "merciless therapy" (the title of one of his books meant to provoke the exponents of academic medicine) was relentlessly attacked by many of his colleagues. And the running boom with the tendency to transfer marathons

[3] https://medical-dictionary.thefreedictionary.com/supercompensation

into the cities was just at the beginning. Not infrequently did doctors not even try to find out the cause of the injury. For them, the cause of the complaints was running itself, which at that time was not necessarily regarded as beneficial to health, and so the medical advice usually was "Stop running!"

To avoid this 'death sentence', runners often consulted each other and read journals such as "Runner's World" to educate themselves on how to solve the medical problems a runner might face.

Nowadays it is much easier to find runner-friendly physicians who also understand something about the matter, because the general social and personal benefits of endurance sports, especially slow jogging and walking, are being propagated everywhere now and have become scientifically substantiated.

Today, you no longer have to worry that your doctor will not do anything apart from telling you to quit running - rather the opposite is the case: often too much is recommended by doctors, for instance when you consult an orthopedist because you have knee problems and he suggests an operation to provide you with an endoprosthesis, an artificial knee joint.

In general, as an experienced runner and running coach, I can give you the following tips for workouts that minimize the likelihood of an injury:

- ✓ The 'bread-and-butter' workout is the slow continuous run with a pulse rate of 110 to 130 (or running at "speech test pace").
- ✓ Long-distance runners are often obsessed with training, with working out. At least one rest day per week is a must!
- ✓ Anyone who realizes that running leads to problems ought to consider that there are alternatives to running.

Workout Alternatives

Cycling

Personally, I have made very good experiences with cycling. I think it is ideal to combine cycling and running, e. g. cycling fast for half an hour and then running in a relaxed manner for half an hour. The combinations of cy-cling and running can be manifold depending on your fitness level and your training goal. It is important that the training session is concluded with running, because then the 'main sport' remains best in the 'muscular memory'.

Kick Biking[4] or Scooter Driving

The author at the beach in Grado / Italy

---

[4] https://kickbike.com/

Kick biking or scooter driving[5] is not yet very popular in the United States and in Germany as against countries such as the Czech Republic, the Netherlands, Italy, etc. Kickbiking is so to speak a mixture of running and cycling. However, it is much more fitness-effective than cycling, because when scootering you easily reach a heart rate of 120 beats per minute. With cycling such a heart rate is only achievable if you push on the pedals really hard. Moreover, with foot biking calorie consumption is much higher since the arms and the trunk of the body are more involved in the exercise process than they are in cycling. Compared to running, the joints, above all the knees and hips, are far less strained.

Aqua Jogging[6]...

... means 'running' in the water with the help of a kind of 'belt' (floatation belt) that allows you to float in the water. I have tried that too. It is very effective, because it's exhausting as you move your arms and legs against

---

[5] sometimes also called foot biking
[6] https://www.theguardian.com/lifeandstyle/the-running-blog/2016/may/11/aquajogging-how-when-and-why-to-try-it

the resistance of the water. What does not make me a fervent supporter of this sport, is the boredom that afflicts me in the pool. As for me, this also applies to swimming in lanes. Therefore, I do not list swimming here as 'substitute gratification' for running, but for those runners who love water, swimming is unquestionably a highly recommendable alternative to running in case of an injury or in a period of recuperation.

Stepper Bike and Elliptigo[7]

The author on a stepper-bike ...

[7] https://www.elliptigo.com/

I am particularly fond of the Elliptigo as an alternative training tool: it is like running (on a bike) without having the impact of pounding on the asphalt with your feet. It is a very effective training with a pulse rate as in running.

Fitness Studio and Treadmill

If you live in a big city or in winter, when the streets and parkways are icy and slippery, the fitness studios that have mushroomed out of the ground are a great alternative to running outdoors.

I have lived in Cairo for five years and running on the streets of this city is not advisable because of the absurdly heavy traffic and because of the very individual, daring driving style of the Arabian motorists[8] and, because of the polluted air there.

In this situation, I chose the alternative of the gym. The treadmills of the "Gold's Gym"[9] were high-tech equipment that allowed speeds of up to 20 km/h, up to 15% inclines, and downhill gradients up to 3%. In addition, the treadmills generally have a very joint-friendly running surface, which seems, at first glance, like an ideal thing - if it had not been for the boredom! Even the view of the pyramids of Gizeh did not make up for the fact that you were running but did not leave the spot. Only after I got the idea of watching movies on a television screen while running, did the treadmill become tolerable for me.

Many running consultants and coaches advise runners to use fitness equipment for muscle-building. I myself

---

[8] However, they claim to be the best car drivers on the planet (among other things).
[9] https://www.goldsgym.com/maadieg/

would not necessarily endorse that because through strength training muscles are formed which you actually do not need for running. On the contrary, the extra body mass makes you heavier and slower and running becomes harder when you weigh more. I think this is an undisputed fact. With strength training, I assume, it is like the British runner Ron Hill[10], a sub-2:10 marathoner, is supposed to have claimed: *The only gymnastics and strength training a runner needs are twenty sit-ups after running. This would stretch the back muscles and strengthen the abdominal muscles. That is all a runner needs as far as strength training is concerned.*

Race Walking and Powerwalking

Race walking is an Olympic discipline in which, unlike running, there must not be any loss of foot contact with the ground – at least not visible for the human eye. In addition, the supporting leg has to be stretched when the heel lands on the ground - i. e. the knee must not be

---

[10] https://en.wikipedia.org/wiki/Ron_Hill

bowed (rule 230 of the ICR - International Competition Rules). This, in particular, leads to the well-known striking hip swing which is sometimes mocked at.

I have also tried this sport, but for me, it was mainly the rule that the knee must be stretched that prevented me from being engaged in race walking any further. I have always found the knee stretch to be very unnatural and uncomfortable. To me modern race walking is nothing more than a kind of stiff-legged running. In my opinion the rule that one leg must always be on the ground is no longer properly controlled or controllable in elite sports. The human eye is simply unable to cope with the enormous step frequency of the elite race walkers.

Powerwalking is athletic walking without the rule of the above-mentioned knee stretching. Powerwalking is already a competitive sport in the US and I think this sport will soon take root in Europe, too, because it comes very close to running and but is less demanding on the joints than running. There are basically two rules in powerwalking: One foot must always remain on the ground and the front (supporting) leg must touch the ground with the heel first.

A very good video clip explaining the difference between race and powerwalking can be found on YouTube: https://www.youtube.com/watch?v=cVkXYYtKFew

Here is some additional expert information that might be of interest[11]:

[...]

Race Walking Techniques

Competitive racewalking dates back to the late 1700s, [...]. Today, there are races all over the world. The 2012 Olympics included 20-km walks for men and women and a 50-km walk for men. Race walkers can reach more than 8 mph, but their activity is very unnatural. Race walking has two rules. One rule requires that one of your feet must be touching the ground at all times. This means that the heel of your front foot must touch the ground before your back foot comes off the ground. The

---

[11] quoted from: https://healthyliving.azcentral.com/race-walking-vs-power-walking-7783.html

second rule requires your front foot's knee to be straight from the time your front foot's heel touches the ground until the rest of your body passes over that leg.

[…]

Power Walking Techniques

The 'walking speed limit for regular walking' is approximately 4.5 mph, […]. Regular walking is a natural activity. Power walkers, though, can reach 5.5 mph by consciously changing their posture, taking faster steps, and swinging their arms. If you want to power walk, you should walk so upright that your head is level and only your eyes move when you look at your feet. You should 'walk as tall as you can,' […]. Taking 135 to 150 steps per minute will improve your speed more than longer strides, which can strain your buttocks, hamstrings and lower back. Swinging your arms while they are bent 90 degrees and your elbows are in a fixed position will also improve your speed.

[…]

More serious Injuries

I was so excited about running because the perception, the experience of the fitness level I achieved through running felt so good that I almost became addicted to it - but this is a positive addiction, I thought to myself and I still think so. By taking up running I managed to reduce my weight from well over 80 kg (176 lbs) at a body height of 1.82 m (5.97 ft) to 67 kg (148 lbs). This allowed me to run very fast and easily without much effort. Gliding almost effortlessly over the asphalt is a fantastic, uplifting and almost sublime feeling. But what looks so easy and elated, does not come by itself, there are many hours of training runs behind it.

I do not believe in the saying "No pain, no gain"[12] as far as training sessions are concerned, because pain surely is no motivating factor. I do not believe that painful training leads to success. On the contrary: if your work-

---

[12] Things are different if we talk in terms of competition. If you want to be victorious in a race, you will have to dig deep and you must be able to tolerate pain, a lot of pain. But the elation, the joy that winning a race brings about is worth it – that is what winners claim.

outs are too hard, too strenuous, you will damage your body and you will end up sidelined by injury. This is my personal experience and I have also observed that with

Certificate of my first marathon at Nuremberg in 2:32:52 on Nov 1, 1981

numerous fellow runners.

In the first year when I began running systematically, I initially increased my running kilometers to about 80 per week. On top of that, I cycled 45 to 60 minutes almost every day - on the bike ergometer when the weather was bad, or, on the road bike when the weather was fine. Tempo training or interval training was not on the program at all, the fast running units were reserved for the competitions. This allowed me to get by completely without injury.

After about 18 months of systematic training I managed to run a 2:32 marathon at Nuremberg (cf. picture on the previous page).

Then came the ambition to run even faster: I changed my running club and began to include speed- and interval-training in my workouts. In retrospect, I can say that was a big big mistake.

Why?

In the following years of hard training I only improved by a few minutes to 2:26 over the marathon, although I increased my mileage per week to 80 or more. I gave up cycling almost completely, I became a pure runner. The reasons why I was able to increase my performance only to a small extent can be summarized in two points:

1. I had left the 'virtuous' path of slow long-distance running as the foundation of my training and had 'swallowed' the poison of interval-training and tempo runs. Dr. van Aaken had already found that it is endurance training which leads to increased performance in the long term, whereas interval training does the opposite because it leaves you tired and overstrained from the many very fast, short outbursts of running that burden the ligaments and tendons much more than the steady motions of the endurance run.

2. I had disregarded the warning signals of my body, i. e. pains, and kept on running for fear of losing my form by taking a break from training. What an error!

The consequences of this wrong training method and attitude showed in the form of various injuries:

- **Inflammation of the abdominal and pyramidal muscles** (adductors)

  This injury has lately frequently appeared among soccer players. Arjen Robben from Bayern Munich, for example, had to fight with it for many months - despite optimal medical care. I had been dealing with that for almost two years. My main mistake was that, despite the pain, I kept on training and even took part in races. Only when I drastically reduced the training load and employed extreme stretching (adductors), did I get rid of this very persistent injury.

- **Haglund exostosis**

  This is a kind of 'extra bone growth' at the back of the heel. Due to an increase in mileage and resorting to interval and speed training, the heel so to say forms a kind of 'reinforcement', a bump that consists of bone and cartilage tissue. This tissue builds up under the Achilles tendon. While running, the tendon rubs over this tissue and becomes inflamed. When that happens, you will suffer excruciating pains that make running impossible. First, you might try conservative methods, such as shock wave therapy, stimulation currents, acupuncture and the like. Yet, my experience is that this is all a waste of time and money. The only thing that helps is an operation in which the tendon is lifted and the tissue that has formed underneath is scraped off.

Why Exactly Running or Walking and Not Another Sport?

I have been asked this question very often and my answer is absolutely personal, others may see things quite differently.

It does not take very much to be a runner/walker: there must be the will to leave the couch and move your body, but apart from the willpower, you only need a pair of good shoes.

I will be discussing in one of the following chapters what I consider to be good running shoes. As a matter of fact, you do not need anything else. Paths, streets, roads, running tracks are to be found everywhere. You can jog on the sidewalks in the city, on the asphalt of the streets, in the woods, on lawns or on the track in the stadium. It is the simplicity and the naturalness of running/walking that have always fascinated me. If necessary, you can also run barefooted, in fact you do not need any sports equipment at all to practice this sport. Barefooted running would probably be the healthiest thing in the world, but our environment and our evolution as human beings has restricted this most natural form of locomotion.

For cycling you need a bike the price of which knows no limits. For racing bikes, you can easily put down 10,000 to 20,000 dollars, for good running shoes you pay between 70 and 150 dollars.

For tennis I need shoes, a tennis court and a partner. As for running, I can run alone, although I have to admit that running is more enjoyable in a group.

If you ride a bike for half an hour, you have done much less for your fitness than after a half-hour run.

Running is so straightforward and effective, with little effort you can achieve amazing results in terms of fitness and health.

What is more, the simplicity and naturalness of running and walking appeal to me aesthetically. I find runners/walkers beautiful.

People have told me that I have an extraordinarily nice running style, so I dare to show some photos of myself as a runner (at different stages of my life as a runner) at the end of this chapter.

I have often used autosuggestion while running and have internally repeated to myself the formula "I am running smoothly and effortlessly, smoothly and effortlessly". This has helped me a lot. By the way, it is scientifically proven that your internal verbalization of thoughts influences your actions decisively.

During marathon races, I often had the picture of a runner who I admired a lot in my mind's eye: the Dutchman Gerald Nijboer, who had won the marathon race at the Euro-pean Championships in Athens in 1982. I had watched the race on TV and admired how easily and fluently Gerald Nijboer mastered the hilly course. That, too, was a little trick I used, so as

The author during a 5K track race in the 1908s

40

not to start counting the miles during the marathon, which can drive you nuts and demotivate you.

Some more pictures from the various stages of the author's life as a runner:

Frequently Asked Questions

During the many running meets that I held at schools and in sports clubs, certain questions kept coming up again and again. I shall try to answer them to the best of my knowledge and conscience.

Should I stretch before running/walking?

To be honest, opinions are quite different here, not unanimous at all. I know good runners who do not stretch at all, because they consider stretching risky and , to my mind, they are not all wrong. If you do not stretch properly, you can actually hurt yourself, for example provoke muscle tears. The latest state of the discussion on this issue, as far as I know it, is as follows:

Before you start running there ought to be something that is called mobilization or warm-up phase. It might look like this: first, you walk a few hundred meters, then move into a slow jog, which also extends over a few hundred meters. Then insert a couple of slight accelerations and maybe some skippings before you hit the planned running pace.

Another variant of mobilization that I have used frequently is running on the spot for a minute or two, followed by rotations of the arms, then hip, knees, and feet. Thus, the shoulder, pelvic and leg areas are prepared for the upcoming load. Before a competition, the warm-up program is a little more extensive and in addition to the warm-up the planned race pace should also be targeted in a couple of acceleration runs. But: never do any stretching exercises before the competition. As it has been found out, this is counterproductive because it affects the muscle tone, which is important in competition. Moreover, after the competition you should not stretch because then the risk of injury is high. Only on the day after the race, should you carefully and gently stretch the strained muscles, tendons and ligaments.

Stretching after a training run, however, is mandatory from my point of view because running strengthens your back muscles, thus making them thicker, and thicker muscles become shorter and can cause problems if they squeeze the discs together. That is why it is clear to me that you should especially stretch the back and leg muscles after a training run.

At which pulse rate should I exercise?

This seemingly very simple question is actually a rather complicated one. First, you will have to decide what the training target is. If it is slow running, you do not have to worry much about the pulse since, in that case, the rule of the speech test tempo applies. That is to say you jog at a pace that makes it possible for you to talk to others without getting breathless while exercising.

There are very complicated formulas for finding out the optimal exercise heart rate for various levels of training, but basically you are on the safe side if you use the following formula: *180 minus your age*. For example, if you are 65 years old, the optimal average heart rate during a training run is around 115 beats per minute.

In any case it is essential that you see a doctor for a complete body check-up before you start running seriously and regularly.

How often and how long should one train / run per week?

Another question to which there is no single, definite and 'correct' answer.

As for beginners, it is my experience that they should run two to three times a week for about 20 to 30 minutes, alternating with walking and slow jogging at the very beginning, e. g. three minutes walking, then two minutes slow jogging. And that up to six times in a row. The walking breaks are reduced gradually and the running intervals are increased until you reach 30 minutes of slow jogging. These 30 minutes of jogging can then be extended by mixed walking and running stretches.

A rule of thumb is that you should increase the amount of training per week by a maximum of 10%. That sounds reasonable to me.

I also recommend to beginners not to run three times a week but to replace one running unit by a powerwalking unit or a bike ride. This is the best way to avoid injury.

For the more advanced runner, who occasionally wants to participate in a race over 5 or 10K, I suggest running three to a maximum of six times a week. Ideally, a basic weekly plan might look like this: one long unit of up to 20 kilometers, a medium-range one over 12 to 16 kilometers and four shorter runs of 6 to 8 kilometers. I do not recommend tempo runs or doing fast intervals, especially not for veteran runners.

Runs at race pace should primarily be reserved for races.

However, what you can do and should do in preparation for the race you want to take part in is that you throw in a couple of crescendo runs into your training sessions. A mile is an ideal distance for such a run: starting with slow jogging you increase the speed of your run every 400 meters until you reach the target race speed over the final quarter mile. Like this you will practice your race tempo without straining your body too much.

After a hard training session or after a race it is highly advisable, even for advanced runners, to take a break from running and use other sportive activities for recreative purposes. This will also help you avoid injuries and boredom in exercising.

Which shoes should I use for running or walking?

Firstly, the good news: nowadays, there are many manufacturers, who all produce high-quality, really good running shoes. That was completely different when I started running back in 1980/81 because then the running scene in Europe was still in its infancy. Long-distance runners were considered exotic, the market for running shoes was small and thus less lucrative for the manufacturers. In the USA, Frank Shorter had won a gold medal at the Olympic marathon in Munich, which launched a wave of enthusiasm for road running in general and marathon running in particular. The NIKE company swam on this wave and became world famous. This 'boom' reached Germany in the 1980s and Nike shoes were in great demand among German runners, although the first specimens available to us rather favored injury than prevented it. In Germany it was mainly two companies that produced good running shoes: Adidas and Brütting, while Puma did not come up with a running shoe I would have used in those days. In recent years, running shoe technology has made enormous progress and there is a virtually unmanageable variety and number of models. Also, Nike and Adidas are no longer alone by now. Other prominent companies have entered this highly profitable market, such as Asics, Mizuno, Hoka One One, Altra, Brooks, Saucony, Under Armor, New Balance, to name just a few of them.

For the selection of the right running shoes it is not the brand name that is crucial but other criteria:

1) **Type of foot**

   If you do not know what type of foot you have,

you can use the so-called wet-foot test which is very simple to do and understand.

The basis of this test is that the wet footstep you leave on the floor while walking is a good indicator on how your foot absorbs the shock of the impact with the floor.

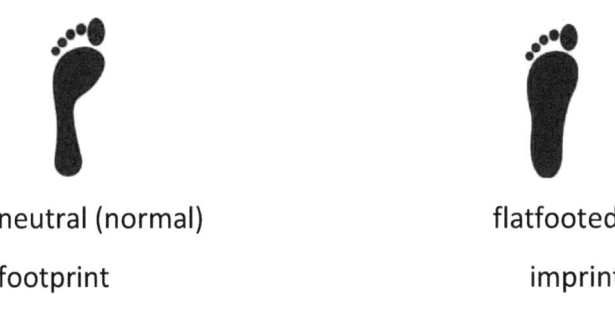

neutral (normal)
footprint

flatfooted
imprint

high-arched footprint

Basically, there are three different foot types: the normal or neutral, the overpronating and the supinating one (cf. above).

'Normal' means that when you strike the floor with your heel, then, while you roll towards the toes, your arch slightly collapses inward absorbing the impact.

If your foot tends to land on the outside of the heel and roll inwards slightly more than a normal pronator, you might be overpronating (cf. "flat-footed imprint").

If your foot tilts outward, which is rare, this is called supination.

Recommendations for choosing the right shoes:

If you have a normal foot, you can wear so-called neutral shoes, over-pronators usually need a pronation support and supinators analogously need a corresponding protection. Runners with high-arched feet should choose a well-cushioned shoe. The shoe manufacturers categorize their running shoes adequately so that everyone can find the right shoes for themselves.

It seems important to me, too, that the shoes have a good cushioning, especially when running on asphalt.

I advise that you go to a running shoe store that has a treadmill on which you can test the shoes of your choice, because 'the proof of the pudding is in the eating'.

2) **The surface you are running on**

For road running you need a different kind of shoe than for trail running. Running on tarmac surfaces means a lot of pounding for your skeletal system, therefore road running shoes should be well cushioned, as I see it.

The Hoka One One company has launched a new trend and makes the soles of running shoes very thick to achieve an optimum of cushioning without sacrificing the necessary stability of their shoes or making them too clumsy.

I personally am a big fan of their shoes. This new trend is totally contrarious to the 'philosophy' of natural running. Natural-running enthusiasts use minimalist shoes that are lightweight but offer virtually no cushioning. They claim that a cushioned shoe spoils your running style and leads to injuries. Running barefooted or quasi-barefooted, like in a minimalist running shoe, is what your body needs. In my opinion, and as I have experienced it, that is the wrong approach, since the necessary adaptation of our feet and body would take very long and would possibly be accompanied by injuries.

But, generally, I agree, running barefooted is the most natural thing, yet modern man is far away from a natural way of living – whatever this may mean. Therefore, I prefer sensibly cushioned running shoes.

3) **Running style**

I think it is also necessary to consider which running style you have. Are you a 'forefoot', 'midfoot' or 'heel' striker?

I find the first two running styles ideal, because they help to absorb the shock of the landing on the ground when running, thus reducing the impact on the skeletal system.

I always try to convince heel strikers to change their running style - usually in vain, because once you have got accustomed to a certain running style, it is difficult to make any changes.

Anyway, the areas of the shoe that first touch the ground while landing after the 'flying phase' in the running cycle should be particularly well cushioned.

There are a number of other possible criteria, for example whether you are looking for a pair of shoes for training or for competition. The subject of racing flats is very diverse and complicated in itself. Anyone planning for a race will find plenty of advice on the internet or at the running shoe retailer's as to which model is the most suitable for him / her. Yet, for the average runner for whom I have written this little guide, I can say that he /

she does not really need a racing shoe for a race on the road over 5K to the marathon because it is safer to stay with one's trainers. Then the risk of injury is also minimized.

And remember, firstly, running injury-free is the most enjoyable and, secondly, the most successful approach in the long term.

5K Training

Why run a 5K-race? Well, it is an approachable distance for beginners and a speed and stamina test for advanced runners.

The advanced runner does not need to train specifically for this distance, he or she can just use it as a test run in the building-up phase of training for a longer run, e. g. a half marathon or a full marathon.

By the way, the principles and methods of training I am presenting here, are equally valid for any kind of walking. It is only the pace that must be adapted individually.

A training regimen that implies regular participation in 5K races might look like this:

Day	Type of training	Mileage
Sun	Rest	0
Mon	4 to 6 m(iles) easy	5
Tue	2m easy; 1m Crescendo run: ¼ m easy; ¼ m slight accelerated run;	5

	¼ m slight acceleration again; ¼ m at anticipated race pace; 2m easy	
Wed	6m easy	6
Thu	Long run: 10 to 12m	10
Fr	Rest	0
Sat	Crescendo run: 2m easy; 1m accelerated; 1m in anticipated race pace 1m easy; ½ m accelerated; ½ m in anticipated race pace 1m easy	7
Sun	Rest	0
Mon	4 to 6 m easy	5
Tue	Like Mon	5
Wed	Long run: 10 to 12m	10
Thu	Rest	0
Fr	Rest	0

Sat	Warm up (2m)	7
	Race 5K	
	Cool down (2m)	

Please keep in mind that I do not favor interval training with fast bursts and tempo runs at a higher speed than race speed for the reasons I have explained earlier in this booklet.

After a race or after a relatively hard training session, as for example after the Saturday crescendo run, it is a good idea to go for a swim or a bike ride to enhance the recreation process.

10K Training

10K is not twice as hard as a 5k race as one might think. Okay it is twice the distance, that is for sure, but the pace is slower than in a 5K and, generally speaking, it is not the distance that 'kills' you, but the speed.

Basically, training for a 10K follows the same principles as those for a 5K. That is why you can follow the 5K plan with a few alterations:

The long run should be 15 to 20 miles and the crescendo runs should be like this:

- ❖ 2m easy
- ❖ 2m slightly accelerated pace
- ❖ 2m acceleration again
- ❖ 2m at anticipated race pace
- ❖ 2 m easy

Half Marathon

If your aim is to tackle a half marathon, you can well use the basic 5/10K plan again. The long run, however, should be around 20 to 22 miles long. In the week of the half-marathon race, the long run on Wednesday is replaced by the following training unit:

- ❖ 2m easy
- ❖ 2m at anticipated race pace
- ❖ 2m easy

Generally, the longer the race distance is, the more important becomes the long jog in the training and the days of rest before the race.

The Marathon

Main Target: To Get Through Well

I have completed about 20 marathons in my running career, the fastest one at Kandel in Rhineland-Palatinate, when I finished in two hours and 26 minutes plus a few seconds, the slowest and last one in about 3 ½ hours twelve years later in Stockholm, when I was not training systematically any more but had become more of a casual runner. In preparation for the marathon at Kandel I ran on average 130 kilometers per week, with at least two tempo units per week. Preparing for Stockholm I covered from around 30 to 60 kilometers a week. In other words, those who aim for the marathon and simply want to get along easily should run three to four times a week and increase their mileage up to 50 during the preparation for the marathon. With fewer miles on your 'account' you will be able to manage, to get along, but it might get really hard and you might harm your body, possibly your soul too, because a marathon is kind of emotional.

When I ran the Stockholm Marathon in 1998 with a minimum preparation of mostly 25 miles per week and a single long run of 20 miles in the preparatory phase, my legs ached terribly during the last few miles and I felt like running on stilts.

When I had run a marathon in the 2:30 hour range with a preparation of over 79 miles per week on average, I was able to run the day after the marathon, as if nothing had happened.

This clearly shows that the marathon is all about 'mile-eating'. If you have more training miles in your legs, things simply become easier.

However, in this case, too, the "law of diminishing marginal utility" applies, which means that there is an upper limit for reasonable improvements.

Marathon runners in particular have to learn to listen to their bodies and, if they perceive warning signs, usually in the form of pain, must react because marathon running and also training for a marathon are so to speak similar to riding on the edge of a razor blade.

For those who just want to get through the marathon, it is important to find a regular rhythm of training and to make long runs of up to 25 miles an integral part of their training.

You can easily predict your probable finish time by using either of these two well-tested and reliable formulas:

a) *10K-PR *4.66* (personal record over 10K multi-plied by 4.66)

I live in Lower Bavaria, Germany. Before the regional marathon championships in 1982 that were scheduled for the end of October to avoid warm weather conditions, I decided to run a test run of 10K, because I wanted to find out if my training was fruitful, i. e. if I was on the right track and could possibly set a new PR for the 10 K. Well, the finish time was not a new PR, but I was also satisfied with the 32 minutes and 12 seconds that I achieved. Two weeks later I ran the marathon in 2 hours 30 minutes and eight seconds. That was almost exactly my 10K finish time multiplied by 4.66.

b) *HM*2 + 10 minutes* (half-marathon finish time multiplied by 2 plus 10 minutes)

This formula is as reliable as the previous one.

On The Hunt For New PR's

If you are on the hunt for personal bests, you will enter dangerous territory. Dangerous insofar as, in my opinion, competitive sport is not necessarily good for your health. Whoever is out for personal records, must go to the limits of physical performance and prepare himself in training for it. The path between what the body can cope with and what becomes too much for it is very narrow, in other words, whoever is engaged in high-performance sports risks his health.

This is, as I have mentioned before, the reason why I have made up my mind to write this booklet. I have made many mistakes myself and with this booklet I am offering you the chance to learn from those mistakes and not to make them again.

I damaged my knees through competitive running. The left knee in a cross-country competition, when I stepped into a swamp hole at high speed and tore my inner meniscus. The right one during a sharp cross-country training on hilly, slippery terrain, as I twisted my knee slipping on a wet root and thus tore my inner meniscus again.

However, competitions are very exciting and the salt in the soup of training. To win a race or a championship against tough competition is an almost indescribable feeling, which you can understand only once you have experienced it yourself.

Nevertheless, I think one should carefully consider the risks before taking action. Risky business in terms of running means above all running at high speed and uneven, slippery surfaces. That is why I have come to prefer running on flat roads or stadium tracks in the meantime.

A Word about Training Plans

Training plans are something very subjective because each of us is built differently, motivated individually. "Individual" means as much as indivisible, i. e. not even two people can share a plan wholly, because the plan has to be tailor-made for each individual.

In other words, everyone can coach him-/herself best because he/she should know him-/herself better than anyone else.

Therefore, if you understand the training principles, you can make your own training plans.

Let me epitomize the most important principles here:

- o Jogging, slow runs at speech test tempo are the 'bread and butter' of training
- o 'Variatio delectat' (Latin saying), i. e. variety makes you happy: Do not always think that you have to run to improve your level of fitness, occasionally use other tools that can help you build endurance and stamina, like for instance the bike, the kick-bike or the Elliptigo etc.

Also look for a variety in the choice of running tracks and surfaces. This helps to prevent injuries and training discomfort.

o Insert rest days! During those, the previously mentioned supercompensation takes place, that is to say your body processes the training and prepares itself for increasing demands. He who does not give his body enough rest, inhibits that process and does not become better by training, but rather poorer in performance.

o Think of the mental component in running. For example, you can improve your style and performance by internally saying formulas to yourself, such as "I am running effortlessly and smoothly".

o Try to find like-minded people because together the fun factor is much higher.

A Short Note about Diets

As for diets, I agree with the aforementioned Dr. med. van Aaken, who said that it is not so important what you eat but how much you eat. What he wanted to drive home was that you should not eat too much in order to keep your body weight low. This protects you against the diseases of civilization and also against sports injuries.

As far as alcohol is concerned, I can say that I enjoy drinking one or two beers or a glass of wine in the evenings. Well, seen purely from the angle of performance, it would be better to do completely without alcohol because alcohol contains a lot of calories and could make you gain weight. But higher weight means lower relative oxygen uptake capacity and thus poorer performance.

However, I have never considered running or walking as a merely competitive sport, but as something that I just enjoy and something that belongs to my life, as well as the moderate consumption of alcoholic beverages. As a

runner, I have always had the feeling that I can afford
this 'luxury'.

In a Nutshell

- ➢ Anyone who wants to start running or walking is well advised to take it easy. A lot of beginners tend to power up too fast.

- ➢ Remember the speech test tempo: you ought to be able to talk while running/walking without getting out of breath.

- ➢ Try to keep an upright posture when jogging and walking: do not slouch forward, look straight ahead and keep your arms bent and swinging. Your arm movements have a decisive influence on your leg speed.

- ➢ Those who experiment with different stride lengths will quickly find out which one is the most comfortable for running or walking.

- ➢ Set goals for yourself. They are an important motivational aid.

- ➢ Do not exaggerate exercising. Beginners should always run and walk in turns. In the first few weeks, 20 minutes of running or walking per training session are sufficient after which you can increase the workload slowly to a maximum of 40 to 50 minutes.

➢ Listen to your body: be considerate and do not force yourself to work out when you do not feel like exercising. By the way, if you run to lose weight, mind this: your body burns most fat when exercising moderately.

➢ Drink enough: if you are traveling for more than 45 minutes, you should definitely have something to drink with you. This is what doctors keep telling us. I myself, however do not need any drinks if the workout is not longer than 60 minutes.

➢ Have a running analysis done in a sports shop to find the right pair of shoes for you. They are the most important equipment for walkers and runners.

A Short Epilogue

Even though I was relatively often injured as a runner because I was unreasonable and because I often trained too much and too hard, I can say that running has definitely enriched my life. I have met numerous people through running and have also made a lot of friends. Running has kept me physically and mentally fit, it has always been to me not only a physical activity but also a form of mental hygiene.

In addition to this, to me a good race or a good run is like a work of art. I derive aesthetic pleasure from it.

An offer at last: in case you have any questions considering the topics that I have dealt with in this booklet, feel free to contact me at:

p_wurzer@yahoo.de

"It is never too late
to be
what you
might have been."

George Elliot

Appendix

Example of a 12-week training plan for running the marathon in around 3 hours

A fellow veteran runner, aged 55, came up to me and asked me if I could provide a training plan for him with the aim of running a marathon in under 3 hours. His height was 1.72 m (equals 5 ft 8), his weight 68 kg (equals 149.9 lbs), his maximum weekly training volume 80 km (50 miles), his current best times over 10K ◊ 41:05 min and ◊ 1:26:14 hrs over the half-marathon distance.

I told him the following things in advance:

1. His weight seems a bit too high for a marathoner. Ideal would be something like under 65 kg (143 lbs). How do I get that figure? The rule of thumb for your ideal weight is as follows:

   The centimeters beyond 100 of your body height are calculated as kg. For instance, if you are 180 cm (5 ft 10) tall, we get the figure of 80 kg (176 lbs).

   From this figure we deduct 10% so that we get

the 'ideal' weight of 72 kg (158.7 lbs).

Dr. van Aaken even maintains that you have to deduct 20% to get the optimal weight of the competitive weight of a marathoner.

Applying this formula on the fellow club runner who wanted to run the marathon in less than 3 hrs, this would mean that his optimal weight should be definitely less than 65 kg (143 lbs) instead of his 68 kg (149.9 lbs).

2. 80 km / 50 miles per week is not an impressive mileage if you want to run 42.195 km (26.2 miles) in under three hours. I think that 100 km (about 60 miles) / week would be more adequate.

3. His current personal bests over 10K and the half-marathon are not good enough for his high aim[13].

He said he wanted to give it a try anyway. If it did not work out, it would be no big deal for him.

---

[13] Remember the formulas to predict marathon finishing times by using the PR's of the 10K or HM (cf. p. 62 f.):
10K-PR *4.66 (personal record over 10K multiplied by 4.66) and *HM*2 + 10 minutes* (half-marathon finish time multiplied by 2 plus 10 minutes)

This is, as I see it, a sound attitude and so I made him a 12-week plan. The marathon was scheduled for mid-October, so the marathon preparation had to start in mid-July, that is to say in the middle of the hot summer months. I took that into account when planning the layout, insofar as I included a lot of cycling or a combination of cycling and running in the plan.

Running when it is hot is very demanding and puts a heavy burden on your body but preparing for a marathon also means that you have to put in quite a few miles on the road no matter what the weather is like. The body gets used to the high temperatures as time passes by and also adapts to those circumstances but to adequately consider this in a training plan is a tricky business. Cycling in hot weather is far less strenuous and, according to my own experience, combined with running helps to avoid injuries without affecting the development of endurance and stamina. In addition, cycling has a proven regenerative function.

The amount of training is calculated in TE (training units), i. e. 1 km of running = 1 TE and 3 km cycling = 1 TE; thus three kilometers of cycling equal one kilometer of running.

Here is the plan in detail:

Weeks 1-4:
<ul><li>Mon: rest (r)</li><li>Tue: 90 min. cycling (c) / ca. 40 km + 30 min. endurance run (er) / ca. 6 km</li><li>Wed: crescendo run (cr): 4 km averaging 5:45 min./km, 4 km - 5:15, 4 km - 4:45e, 4 km - 4:15 (= target race pace), 2 km cooldown.</li><li>Thu: 45 min. c + 45 min. er</li><li>Fri: r</li><li>Sat: 20 km er</li><li>Sun: 2 hrs. c + 60 min. er</li></ul>

At the end of the 4th week there is a test race over 10 K or a test run with clubmates. Cycling and running result in a weekly workload of 91 TE, which is more than the desired eighty running kilometers, but since cycling is less of an orthopedic and also organic burden to the body, this roughly equals 80 km of purely running.

Weeks 5-8
• Mon: r
• Tue: 20 km er
• Wed: crescendo run (cr): 4 km averaging 5:45 min./km, 4 km - 5:15, 4 km - 4:45e, 4 km - 4:15 , 2 km cooldown;   → alternatively: 3K or 5K test run
• Thu: 60 min. c + 30 min. er
• Fri: 45 min. er
• Sat: local race of up to 10K
• Sun: 60 min. c + 2 hrs. s(low) j(ogging) - 24 km

Weekly total → ca. 95 TE

Weeks 9-10

- Mon: r
- Tue: 60 min. c + 45 min. er
- Mi: cr
- Thu: 45 min. c + 60 min. er
- Fri: r
- Sat: HM → finish time 1:27, hot weather conditions
- Sun: 60 min. c + 30 min. sj
- Mon: r
- Tue: 60 min. sj
- Wed: 60 min. c + 60 min. sj
- Thu: like on Tue
- Fri: r
- Sat: like on Wed
- Sun: 35 km sj

Wochen 11-12

- Mon: r
- Tue: 60 min. c
- Wed: 60 min. sj
- Thu: as on Wed
- Fri: r
- Sat: 30 min. sj + 5 acceleration runs (ar) of ca. 150 m
- Sun: 10K race → 39:15[14] min. windy conditions but not warm
- Mon: r
- Tue: 10 km sj
- Wed: warmup, 5 km in 12:45 min, cooldown
- Thu: 30 min. sj + 5 ar (150 m)
- Fri: r
- Sat: 20 min. sj + 5 ar (150 m)
- Sun: Marathon → under 3:00:00 hrs?

---

[14] New PR: an improvement of almost 2 minutes compared to the previous PR

Unfortunately, the day of the marathon was not exactly my protégé's lucky day. During the marathon he had to fight with temperatures of well over 20 degrees centigrade (more than 70 degrees Fahrenheit), so that the targeted finish time was soon like a fata morgana but up to the half marathon mark he was fully on course. Unfortunately, when he passed this mark, the sun was highest …

Interim times achieved:	
• 5 km	0:20:03
• 10 km	0:41:44
• 15 km	1:03:02
• 20 km	1:24:16
• HM	1:28:59
• 25 km	1:46:19
• 30 km	2:08:44
• 35 km	2:33:36
• 40 km	3:03:34
• Finish	3:15:20

It is obvious that the collapse came at the 35K mark - something that often happens in the marathon, which is notoriously known as 'hitting the wall' or "meeting the man with the hammer", as we put it over here.

This occurs when the body's glycogen stores are exhausted and the body then metabolizes fat to create energy. You easily hit the wall when you're traveling too fast for the first few miles, which also was the case with my protégé. In the initial euphoria of the marathon fever he ran the first 5K more than a minute faster than scheduled and that was what he had to pay the price for in the end. He had also chosen the wrong pair of shoes: instead of taking the light trainers he had been accustomed to from the long runs, he picked his racing flats which he used in 5K and 10K road races. They earned him hot feet on the even hotter asphalt, which partly gave him the feeling of running over burning ashes. Then he only drank water during the race, which I think is wrong because it can give you the feeling of an empty stomach and so lead to the phenomenon of "hitting the wall" prematurely. I strongly advise not to drink only water but also the electrolytes offered, which might help you avoid emptying your glycogen stores.

A Word of Thanks

First and foremost, I would like to thank my wife Traudi,

who also used to run, but has now more turned to Nordic Walking.

She has always been very

My wife Traudi next to me on the left-hand side after a race

supportive to me and I am sure I would not have become a national class runner without her.

Then I want to thank my son Robert for providing me

with very useful feedback when I was writing this booklet.

My son Robert and myself after a common training run

Last but not least, a big "Thank You" to my dear friend and former fellow teacher **Edgar Schaffner**, who proof-read my book and who gave me a lot of helpful hints.

"Methinks that the moment
my legs began to move,
my thoughts began to flow."

Henry David Thoreau